Think Like a Scientist at the Beach

by Dana Meachen Rau

ERRY L

Published in the United States of America by Cherry Lake Publishing
Ann Arbor, Michigan
www.cherrylakepublishing.com

Content Editor: Robert Wolffe, EdD, Professor of Teacher Education,
Bradley University, Peoria, Illinois

Design and Illustration: The Design Lab

Photo Credits: Page 4, ©MaszaS/Shutterstock, Inc.; page 8, ©Lisa F.
Young/Shutterstock, Inc.; page 10, ©Willyam Bradberry/Shutterstock,
Inc.; page 15, ©ClimberJAK/Shutterstock, Inc.; page 17, ©Mary Evans
Picture Library/Alamy; page 20, © John Wollwerth/Shutterstock, Inc.;
page 21, ©iStockphoto.com/HultonArchive; page 26, ©Johanna
Goodyear/Shutterstock, Inc.; page 27, ©Greenland/Dreamstime.com;
page 28, ©Media Bakery; page 29, ©WDG Photo/Shutterstock, Inc.

Library of Congress Cataloging-in-Publication Data
Rau, Dana Meachen, 1971 –
  Think like a scientist at the beach/by Dana Meachen Rau.
      p. cm.—(Science explorer junior)
  Includes bibliographical references and index.
  ISBN-13: 978-1-61080-168-3 (lib. bdg.)
  ISBN-10: 1-61080-168-7 (lib. bdg.)
  1. Beaches—Juvenile literature. 2. Coast changes—Juvenile literature.
I. Title. II. Series.
  GB453.R38 2011
  551.45'7—dc22   2011001405

Cherry Lake Publishing would like to acknowledge the work
of The Partnership for 21st Century Skills. Please visit
www.21stcenturyskills.org for more information.

Printed in the United States of America
Corporate Graphics Inc.
July 2011
CLFA09

TABLE OF CONTENTS

How Does That Work?

There are many things to study at the beach.

Have you ever looked at something and wondered, "How does that work?" Scientists do that all the time. Even at the beach.

You could study sailboats at a beach.

Next time you are playing in the sand or splashing in the water, ask questions like a scientist. How does a boat float? Why does the sand change along the shore? How does a towel get dry? **Geology**, **biology**, and **physics** are just a few kinds of science you can use to answer your questions about the beach.

You can get your own answers by thinking like a scientist. Go step by step. You may have to repeat some steps as you go.

1. Observe what is going on.
2. Ask a question.
3. Guess the answer. This is called a **hypothesis**.
4. Design an **experiment** to test your idea.
5. Gather materials to test your idea.
6. Write down what happens.
7. Make a **conclusion**.

Don't forget your notepad!

Use words and numbers to write down what you've learned. It's okay if an experiment doesn't work. Try changing something, and then do the experiment again.

Remember to take careful notes as you work.

GET THE FACTS

Libraries have information about any subject you can think of.

Scientists look for facts before they start an experiment. They use this information as a place to start.

Where can you find information? A library is filled with books, magazines, and science videos that can help you. A great place for research is in the field. If you live close enough, try to visit a beach or an aquarium.

You can also find facts on the Internet. Be careful. Not everything on the Internet is the truth. Ask an adult to help you find the best places to look for information.

An aquarium is a good place to learn about animals and plants that live in oceans.

Castle Attack!

What causes some waves to be taller than others?

Watch the waves. They come in and they go out, over and over again. About twice each day, the waves creep slowly up the beach covering more and more sand. This is called high tide. Then the water moves back again, showing more sand at low tide.

Do the waves carry anything away? Do they leave anything behind? How does the sand change as the waves wash over the beach? Make a guess. This is your hypothesis.

Hypothesis: Waves take away sand and leave behind shells or seaweed.

Make a hypothesis based on what you already know.

DO AN EXPERIMENT

Wait for low tide and build a sand castle. All you need is a pail and shovel. Find a flat area a few feet away from the edge of the water. Build up towers of sand with your pail, shovel, and hands. Add a lot of details to your castle.

Your sand castle can be any shape and size you choose.

Now wait for the tide to come in. When the waves start lapping the edge of your castle, look at a watch and write down the time. Observe what happens as the water washes over your sand castle. When it is completely flattened, write down the time again.

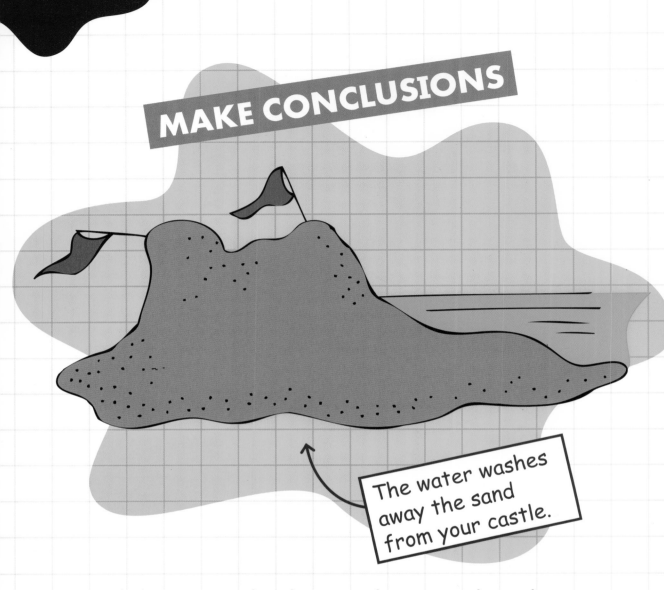

MAKE CONCLUSIONS

The water washes away the sand from your castle.

How did your castle change shape as the tide came in? How long did it take for the waves to flatten your castle? What happened to the sand?

In the 1800s, a British geologist named Charles Lyell observed the way flowing water **eroded** soil.

Look closely at a dune. Do you notice any patterns in the sand?

The water took the soil from one place and dropped it in another. He thought that erosion had been changing Earth for millions of years.

Notice the larger piles of sand called dunes farther from the water's edge. Do you think this sand was shaped by waves? What else might erode sand at a beach? Could wind have something to do with it?

Where Does the Water Go?

People hang towels out to dry. Do you know why?

What happens if you dip your towel into water? That's easy! It gets wet, just like you do if you take a dip. But how does a towel get dry? Where does the water go?

16

Water turns into an invisible gas when it is heated. This is called **evaporation**. The gas goes up in the air and turns into clouds. The clouds drop water back to Earth as rain. A British scientist named John Dalton studied this water cycle. The conclusions to his experiments helped us understand more about evaporation.

John Dalton was born in England in 1766.

TRY AN EXPERIMENT

Make sure you get all three towels wet.

Your hypothesis for this experiment could be: water will evaporate best in the sun. Now test your idea! You need three towels to test evaporation. Make sure they are all the same size and kind of towel. Dip the towels into the water until they are soaked. Then wring out the towels to get out the extra water. The towels will still be very wet!

Open one towel and lay it across the back of a beach chair. Put that chair in the bright sun. Open and lay another towel on the back of a chair. Put that chair in the shade of an umbrella. Place the last towel in a plastic bag. Wait for about an hour.

Check the towels. Which one is dry? Which one is still wet? Why do you think you got these results?

You can explore something else at the beach while you wait an hour to check on the towels.

Sink Like a Stone

Archimedes made discoveries that help explain why a surfboard doesn't sink.

If you toss a rock into the water, it probably sinks to the bottom. A surfboard is a lot bigger than a rock. But it floats on the surface.

Archimedes, a Greek mathematician, studied how objects act in water. He noticed that when an object was placed into water, the water level rose. The object **displaced**, or pushed aside, some of the water.

If you put an object in water, the object pushes down on the water. The water pushes up on the object, too. That's why things float. Archimedes stated that the force pushing up on an object in water is equal to the weight of the water the object displaces. The force of the water pushing up is called **buoyant force**.

Archimedes was born in about 287 BCE in Syracuse, Sicily.

Some objects sink. Let's explore why.

If a buoyant force pushes up on objects, why do some objects sink? To know if an object will sink or float, you have to know how dense it is.

Weight is how heavy something is. Volume is how much space something takes up. If something weighs a lot but takes up only a little space it has a high density. Something that weighs a little but takes up a lot of space is not as dense. A marble the size of a small marshmallow is heavier than the marshmallow. The marble has a higher **density**.

Scientists have concluded that if an object has a higher density than water, it will sink. If the object is less dense than water, it will float. This is a good hypothesis to check with an experiment.

Hypothesis: If an object is less dense than water, it will float.

Do you agree with this hypothesis?

TRY AN EXPERIMENT

Collect a large rock, a shell, and a piece of wood from the beach. Drop the rock onto the sand. What happens? Next, drop the shell and, finally, the piece of wood. They should all drop straight down to the ground.

You can experiment with objects you find at the beach.

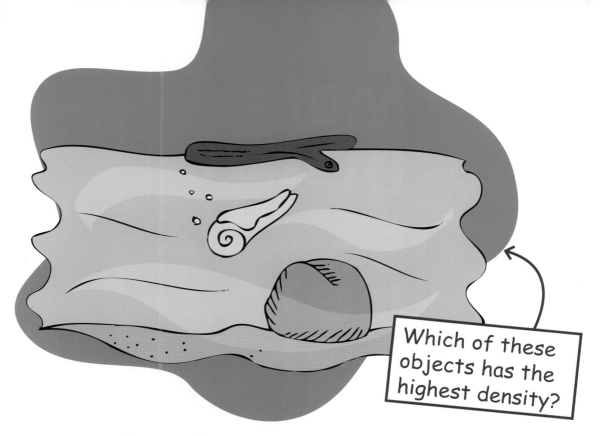

Which of these objects has the highest density?

Now walk into the water up to your waist. Drop the same rock, shell, and piece of wood into the water. What happens? Write down your observations.

You may notice the objects act differently than they did on land. The rock probably sinks. The shell might sink, too, but it will take a little longer to hit bottom than the rock did. The wood probably floats on top of the water. From your results, what do you conclude about the density of these objects?

More to Discover

Many of the rocks you find on a beach are very smooth. Do you wonder why?

An experiment does more than just answer your hypothesis. It often makes you think of more questions to ask.

You have tested how waves change the land. Does this help explain why beach rocks are so smooth? What kind of experiment could you do to find out?

You know that water evaporates. What will happen if you put salty ocean water on a plastic plate and leave it in the sun? Will anything be left on the plate after the water evaporates?

Does salt water leave anything behind when it evaporates? Try an experiment!

THINK LIKE A SCIENTIST

Explorer Jacques Cousteau was born in France in 1910.

Ocean explorer Jacques Cousteau spent much of his life observing the creatures of the sea. You can watch the animals, too.

Notice how seagulls glide in the air. Watch how a sandpiper pokes in the sand. How are their bodies built for life at the beach? Dive under water to spy a fish darting past. Why doesn't the fish sink or float? Maybe it has something to do with density!

Observe, ask, and discover. Think like a scientist. Grab your swimsuit, towel, pail, and shovel, and let's head to the beach!

Observe a group of seagulls. What questions do you have about them?

GLOSSARY

biology (bye-AH-luh-jee) the study of living things, including plants and animals

buoyant force (BOI-uhnt FORS) the force pushing up on an object in or under water

conclusion (kuhn-KLOO-zhuhn) the answer or result of an experiment

density (DEN-sih-tee) the mass of an object compared to its size

displaced (dis-PLAYSD) took the place of

eroded (i-ROH-did) broke down or wore away

evaporation (i-VAP-uh-rate-id) the process of water entering the air

experiment (ik-SPER-uh-ment) a test of your idea

geology (jee-OL-uh-jee) the science of the changing land of Earth

hypothesis (hye-PAH-thi-sis) a guess

physics (FIZ-iks) the science of matter and energy

FOR MORE INFORMATION

BOOKS

Bailey, Jacqui, and Matthew Lilly (illustrator). *Cracking Up: A Story About Erosion*. Minneapolis: Picture Window Books, 2006.

Kalman, Bobbie. *Explore Earth's Five Oceans*. New York: Crabtree Publishing Company, 2010.

Mezzanotte, Jim. *How Water Changes*. Milwaukee: Weekly Reader Early Learning Library, 2007.

WEB SITES

Discovery Education—Planet Ocean
school.discoveryeducation.com/schooladventures/planetocean/ocean.html
Learn more about Earth's oceans.

NASA Oceanography
science.nasa.gov/earth-science/oceanography/
Read more about how scientists study oceans.

INDEX

ABOUT THE AUTHOR

Dana Meachen Rau writes and experiments in Burlington, Connecticut. She has written more than 250 books for children.